adventure playgrounds, ten pin bowling or ice skating. A child who likes sport can enjoy going to a sports centre or club with friends after school, or in the holidays. Youth club and after school activities frequently involve sports and physical skills. Being able to have fun together is an important factor in making friendships. Sport and leisure providers have a huge role to play in making sure that the activities offered for children and young people are genuinely open to all.

▧ Case study

David is 14 years of age and has been totally blind since birth. Every week during term time he attends Liverpool and Blackburn Actionnaires clubs for blind and partially sighted young people aged 8 to 16, which have been set up and are run by the charity Action for Blind People. Before this David had no real experience of participating in sport. When he first arrived, David lacked the confidence to participate in the activities being run at the club, such as cricket, judo and goalball.

Initially David required constant one-to-one supervision throughout the sessions. He held someone's hand continuously, and in the beginning, the "running" was more of a shuffle or walk.

David has now developed dramatically. Six months down the line David has learned how to run (correctly). This sounds simple, but for someone who has never been exposed to this type of coaching, his improvement has been remarkable.

David is now able to run on his own, kick a ball and participate in all the team activities that are run at the clubs. This summer he attended a Sports Camp where he took part in kayaking, cricket, football and athletics among other things. On top of this, all the young people took part in a rookie lifeguard award and David passed with flying colours.

At the Actionnaires club David is competing on a level playing field with children of a similar age who come from different schools and backgrounds. David has made friends at the club and he is extremely keen to learn more. He is especially eager to study Martial Arts.

Positive thinking

Children and young people need a variety of opportunities to be physically active. There is a risk that some young people with sight problems become increasingly inactive in their teens, because of their difficulties in participating in the activities of sighted peers. It is therefore particularly important that they should be encouraged to participate in a range of physical activities. Young people should be encouraged to participate in sports, physical activity and recreational pastimes in which they can perform reasonably well, whether alone, with sighted peers or with other young people with sight problems.

The prospect of adapting an activity may at first appear somewhat daunting for a PE teacher or sports coach, but with minor adjustments and a little lateral thinking it can be done. Simple modifications to most activities often provide solutions, which can be developed and adapted according to the needs and enthusiasms of the young person with a sight problem and their sighted peers. However, it is important that the participant who has a sight problem is not unnecessarily singled out.

Skills and experience

Young people with sight problems need to learn skills that help to develop general motor ability and which make it possible for them to engage in a variety of sports. Some sports have specifically adapted versions for participants who have impaired vision. Examples of these include popular games such as cricket, football, judo and rounders, as well as organised athletics and swimming events offering opportunities for people with sight problems to compete against other disabled people. Whatever their physical disabilities, young people with sight problems need concrete experiences which will enable them to understand and contribute to discussions with their sighted peers.

This book looks at how sports coaches and PE teachers can enable young people with sight problems to join in, learn and enjoy. For more on encouraging the development of basic skills see page 11.

Sight problems and sport

It is important not to make general assumptions about a young person's sight problem and abilities.

Many different eye conditions can affect a person's sight and the effects vary widely. Few blind people see nothing at all. Most have some residual sight but this may be blurred or patchy: some people may see at the sides, others only in the centre of their vision. Some see best in good lighting, while others cannot tolerate bright light.

What does it mean?

The main concern of the PE teacher or sports instructor does not necessarily need to be the name of the young person's sight problem, but rather its various functional effects. These may include:

- a reduced ability to see images sharply (visual acuity)

- reduced visual field. Depending on the field loss this might mean that a child may not notice something to one side without turning his head, or not notice things below waist level without looking directly down, or could be less likely to see a ball approaching above eye level

- impaired ocular mobility. This means that the young person is less able to control the movement of their eyes to follow a moving object, or fix on a static target

- low contrast sensitivity. For example, a young person might find it difficult to detect an orange ball being held by a team mate with a red vest, or to see a white ball travelling in a room with cream walls

- poor adaptation to light (including photophobia). This could mean that a young person may need time to adapt to sudden changes in lighting level such as coming out of a dark changing room into a brightly lit sports hall or sunny day. Some students are very sensitive to bright artificial or natural light and some may find it painful. Some students

The importance of sport

© AFBP

Physical activity is important for all children and young people. Young people with sight problems can and do achieve physical fitness and with appropriate support and encouragement many become skilled in a wide range of sporting activities. Sight problems need not be a barrier to developing physical skills and enjoying sport.

Well-organised sport is enjoyable, builds confidence and improves general health and fitness. Young people with sight problems have the same need for activity, challenge, teamwork and competition as fully sighted young people. Children and young people with sight problems have much in common with their sighted peer group, and like them, each is unique with individual likes, dislikes and practical needs. This book is about enabling young people with sight problems to develop physical skills, feel good about themselves, discover their potential and have fun.

Essential information for coaches

This chapter contains essential information that is common to all sporting activities, including the implications of sight problems in the context of sport, safety and good practice.

The next chapter contains information about how to teach children with sight problems the basic physical skills that are the foundation for all other sports. Subsequent chapters provide additional more specific information about enabling children with sight problems to participate and gain success in particular sports. The case studies provide an insight into individual children's experiences such as transferring from primary to secondary school, attending out of school clubs, and studying PE for GCSE.

Starting young

It is important that opportunities for varied and successful sport and leisure activities occur in early childhood, as these experiences can stimulate interests which encourage an active lifestyle throughout adult life. As a first step it is essential that young people with sight problems are given every opportunity to take a full part in physical education at school. Taking part in physical education helps children to build self-esteem, become physically fitter, develop their independence, provides opportunities for social integration and is vital for all-round development. But it is just the first step.

Making it fun

Enabling children to enjoy sport is the ultimate aim. A child who enjoys sport and has a positive attitude to new experiences is more likely to be invited to social events such as birthday treats, many of which involve activities such as swimming, clambering around soft play centres or

Foreword

■ **To children and young people
with sight problems:**

"Hi! My name is Maria Carr and I'm 16 years old.
I live in Huddersfield and run for my local athletics
club, Holmfirth Harriers. I take part in goalball
training at school and play football at an
Actionnaires club on Saturdays at a sports centre.

At college I go rock climbing. I also love dancing -
ballroom and line dancing.

I've had glaucoma and nystagmus since birth and
had one eye removed when I was 13 due to an ulcer.

If you want to take part in a sport don't let anything
stop you. Just go for it, because that is what I did
and I am living my dream."

Contents

may find it helpful to wear a baseball cap and their tinted spectacles in such conditions

- impaired or inconsistent colour vision affects a young person's ability to recognise team vests, the referee, or to carry out instructions relating to coloured sports equipment including mats, bats and balls

- very little or no vision. Some young people with sight problems may rely entirely on verbal descriptions, sounds, echoes and tactile information.

What coaches need to know

For school-based teachers, information about your student's medical condition, including the diagnosis, prognosis and any implications for physical activity, should be available in school records. This is essential information as it relates to safety and influences the way the learning environment needs to be organised. It is often helpful to ask to meet the specialist teacher for children with impaired vision to gain a better understanding of how a young person is able to use their vision in different situations and what factors, if any influence the young person's vision.

If you are a sports coach or leisure provider working in an out of school setting you must gain the same information as outlined in the paragraph above. It is essential for safety. You can seek the information from the young person's parents, perhaps seeking their permission to talk directly to a specialist teacher of children with visual impairment. Check this information carefully.

Young people themselves should also be encouraged to understand the implications of their eye condition and how it will affect their participation in sporting activities. As they get older they will become more able to describe the support they need and to let you know when they want to be more independent.

Wearing glasses

If a child needs to wear glasses to see in PE lessons or out of school sport, do encourage this. It is important that children are able to use the vision they have, and many children feel thoroughly disorientated without their glasses. Wearing glasses is safer for the child and therefore for the rest of the group. The lenses should be plastic and shatterproof. The glasses should fit snugly, and preferably should be secured with a sports band.

If glasses are damaged during PE activities, parents of children under the age of 16 can get help with the cost of replacing them. However, for general day to day PE lessons it is advisable for some children to protect their glasses by wearing a pair of "Over Goggles". Children who are seriously committed to team and contact sports can obtain and wear special prescription sports glasses.

Alternative strategies

Teachers and coaches can help students to develop strategies to cope with or overcome any difficulties. In seeking to design such strategies, account needs to be taken of individual factors in addition to visual functioning. These include:

- physical activity capabilities – past experience, present level of skill acquisition, body type, physical fitness, physical maturity, and posture

- orientation and mobility development – body awareness, spatial awareness, mental mapping, independent movement, ability to orientate themselves

- medical history – whether the young person previously had sight and lost it suddenly, whether it has gradually deteriorated or whether the participant has never had much sight. This has implications for a child's understanding of the physical world and the skills they have developed to gain information through listening and by touch. Some eye conditions may also impose restrictions on certain physical activities. For example, a young person with retinal detachment problems should not do high impact sports such as trampolining, high jump, or diving. Heavy lifting, for example, helping to carry a vault or other heavy apparatus, may also be dangerous for children with certain eye conditions

- cognitive ability – ability to understand and follow instructions, understanding cause and effect, problem solving, tactical awareness, evaluation, ability to use visual clues and auditory clues and reliance on auditory memory

- motivation and interests – fears or inhibitions, interaction with peers, personal and family attitudes, involvement, enthusiasm, confidence.

Safety

Safety is of primary importance when teaching PE or organising sporting activities. The help of an additional adult can be essential in ensuring safety for the whole group. A young person with a sight problem should be made familiar with all the sports facilities, such as changing rooms, gym, sports hall and pool. A safe route to the venue for each physical activity should be planned in advance.

Potential hazards such as unmarked steps, stored equipment, poolside equipment should all be pointed out, and consistency in storage of such equipment should be ensured where possible. Children or young people who have a sight problem must take a full part in the setting up and replacement of equipment as it enables them to gain a better understanding of the equipment used and the layout of the room. Socially it is important that they share the same responsibilities as sighted children in the group. Use of a clear and methodical system and routine is helpful.

In addition, a support staff member should work in partnership with the teacher or coach to ensure safety in the following ways. Make sure that:

- the young person is aware of the specific working area for each activity and that they have knowledge of the exact location of equipment and apparatus

- the young person understands the general safety rules for each activity

- in "jumping off" activities and in the swimming pool, that a young person with sight problems checks specific safety issues such as distance to the ground and proximity to other students

- enough instructions and auditory signals are appropriately given

- safety rules are known and followed by all members of the group

- the lighting conditions are safe to meet with the specific needs of the participant who has a sight problem.

You should also bear in mind that:

- a young person's sight can vary from day to day, according to changing lighting levels, fatigue and with general fluctuations of the eye condition

- vision plays an important part in maintaining balance. Take into account that a lack of vision may therefore affect movement, balance and coordination.

Conclusion

So make it fun. Find out what the young person's sight problem means for the particular sport or activity. Be positive, creative and safe and enable the young person to enjoy successes at each stage.

Case study

Sean Fisher is 16 years old, 6ft 2", represents Cambridge for both rugby and athletics and has been actively involved in a very wide range of sporting activities since he was very little. Last year, he won two bronze medals and a silver in the County Athletics championships, two silver medals in the East of England athletics championships and he was Junior Thrower of the Year for his local athletics club. He has also recently achieved his Duke of Edinburgh Bronze Award. Oh, and he's registered blind!

Sean has aniridia and nystagmus, and does have quite a bit of useful vision but finds it difficult to pick out detail at any distance. In day to day terms, he uses large print and has a support assistant part-time at school.

Sean's parents have always, since he was very little, encouraged his involvement in the activities enjoyed by his peers. Starting with Tumbletots, he has been involved in Beavers, Cubs, Scouts and a range of sports. His parents never relied on school to provide enough sporting activities for Sean, but ensured his social integration by trying out a range of sports in local clubs.

When he was younger, he played football at a local club, until around the age of 10 or 11, the game became too fast for him at a competitive level. He still enjoys a kickabout and loves watching professional football on TV.

He also tried judo, which proved very accessible, apart from the fact that he has always been much taller than his peers, so was matched against 17 year olds when he was only 11!

Then he went along to one of the "Sport for All" taster sessions at a local athletics club and discovered a real talent. Sean specialises in throwing events and can put his hand to hammer, shot and javelin, but discus is his favourite event.

Sean's visual impairment does not place any barriers on his competing.

Rugby is another favourite, and Sean's position is prop. This involves a lot of close-quarters activity, so locating the ball is not a problem.

He finds it, runs with it and throws it to whoever is calling his name! He is also responsible for other elements of the game not dependent on perfect sight such as knocking big men out of the way or lifting other big men in the air to catch the ball!

All of the team know that Sean has a sight problem but it really isn't an issue with them. His team coach has worked with Sean's strengths - height, speed and physical stature and relies on other team members to use their skills in locating the ball when it's out of Sean's visual range.

The rugby ball used by the team is always kept very clean and white so that it's easier for him to spot, and grounds that have decent floodlights can make a real difference to Sean's game.

As Sean's dad says, "I've always been keen to encourage coaches to realise that players don't need to be wonderful at every element of a game to be fantastic within a team. Good coaches encourage the skills that each player has."

Sean is hoping to study PE at A level, and although he hasn't yet decided what he'll do when he leaves school, he's sure to be fit and active for many years to come!

Developing basic skills

Some basic skills are common requirements for many sports.

Being able to control our own body's position and to move it through space requires a complex set of physical skills which we often take for granted. Many children are able to acquire these skills by imitating others, having a go and practising, without much direct teaching. For example, although children are encouraged, most are not strictly speaking "taught" to sit, walk, or run. Some children, however, do need more adult intervention to acquire some of these foundation skills. Some children have difficulties with motor control, and children with sight problems have fewer opportunities to clearly see other people demonstrating these skills. A sight problem can make it harder to be aware of what you need to do differently to get a better result, and can hinder a child's appreciation of other people's work, unless lots of descriptions are given.

The way in which basic physical skills are taught to children throughout their school years, has a profound impact on their likely enjoyment of sport. Some children with sight problems become aware that they are "not as good" at a particular skill as their sighted peers. For some this is discouraging enough for them to "give up" trying. While some give up on a particular skill others feel ready to give up on all things physical. The challenge for PE teachers and sports coaches is to find age-appropriate and fun ways of filling in the gaps, enabling success.

Children with sight problems need to experience safe movement with co-ordination and control. To achieve this they need to develop an understanding of aspects of space and manipulation.

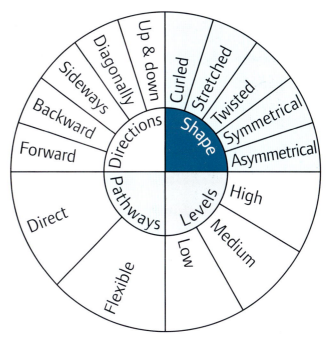

If you are teaching basic physical skills to a group that includes a child with sight problems, ask the following questions:

- what assistance or support is required? Who will provide it?

- what descriptive language does the young person need to understand in order to make sense of clear detailed instructions? For example, does the child understand, left, right, up, down, on, under and through? Has each piece of equipment and area been introduced, named, described and explored?

- what equipment is most suitable for this activity? How can it be made more visible or audible, and what effect will lighting have on the activity?

- how can the environment be adapted? Can a smaller defined quiet area be made to enable the child with sight problems to move more confidently, and be able to hear what is happening?

- how can the skill be broken down into small steps, to ensure the child experiences success?

- how can I adapt the activity? Would it be appropriate for a child with sight problems to be allowed extra time to develop a particular skill rather than to try everything that is planned for the whole group? Can the activity be adapted to give a child with impaired vision greater time to react or complete a move?

Basic skills for dance, movement and music and gymnastics

- Walking
- Running
- Jumping
- Hopping
- Sliding
- Crawling
- Climbing
- Balancing

The teaching points for the above will vary according to each child's age, ability and visual functioning. Allow "failure" to be an acceptable thing and then enable children to work on it. Consider working through the following progressions linked with the "Aspects of space" diagram on page 11:

- support given by an adult hand

- support given by holding a short wooden baton

- link to a partner through short piece of elastic cord with two loops

- use bells on elastic bracelet to follow a partner - use of listening skills

- verbal instructions

- introduce simple low level equipment

- add lots of praise and encouragement.

© Nigel Madhoo

Basic ball skills

Many sports, for example basketball, netball, football and rugby require the development of projecting, throwing and catching skills.

Consider using a "sound ball" or "soft-surface" ball and decide on the most appropriate size and colour of ball for the activity. Balls with different textures or fluorescent colours can also make a big difference.

Projecting skills

Children need to develop their ability to control the ball's direction, speed and its power or force. A young person needs opportunities to develop the following skills:

- manipulative skills appropriate to the size and weight of the ball

- one handed and two handed throwing

- throwing underarm and overarm
- learning to do a back swing - linked to follow through with a straight arm finish
- step into the throw.

For kicking skills children need opportunities to practise using both right and left feet as well as restricted body parts. It is important to provide children with experience of using the inner and outer part of their feet as well as toes.

Catching skills

Many children with sight problems need to be explicitly taught each of the following:

- how to form a curved hand shape ready for catching
- correct positioning of hands in relation to their body
- how to draw the ball into the body as it arrives
- how to protect themselves if a ball is travelling towards them and they realise they are not going to be able to catch it
- how to use clues to judge a ball's direction of travel, speed and power.

Striking skills

If a child has no vision, it can be very difficult to develop striking skills. However, children who are totally blind can have a certain degree of success if they develop very good listening skills and use a "sound ball".

Children who have partial sight often require:

- a larger, slow bounce or flight
- a brightly coloured ball/shuttlecock etc

- a larger striking implement such as a light-weight tennis racket to play badminton
- use of a "ball-support stand" to strike a still ball as distinct from a moving ball
- permission to simply throw the ball rather than strike it eg when it is their turn to bat in rounders.

Consider modifying the rules to cover distance, speed, direction or power. Remember, it is vital that a child who has sight problems experiences success, opportunities to progress and constructive feedback.

Most children will need extra work with co-ordinating the visual tracking of the ball and then connecting it to the back swing, the point of striking and the follow through. Providing lots of verbal support helps.

See other specific sports and activities for further detail.

Angela Brassey
RNIB Advisory Teacher of Visually Impaired Children, PE and Mobility RNIB New College Worcester

■ Case study

Sally, Year 6 - transferring from primary to secondary school

Sally has an eye condition called retinopathy of prematurity which means that her retinas didn't develop well. She also has a cataract in her left eye. With her left eye she can perceive light only. With her right eye she can see at 6 metres what a fully sighted person can see from 18 metres.

Sally is generally a happy child and enjoys her academic work but she is not too keen on PE. This is quite likely to be related to the fact that she is overweight, is not aerobically fit and she finds most physical activity rather arduous.

Sally's teaching assistant has worked hard with her throughout her primary education to encourage Sally to be more physically active.

Sally is confident socially except in PE where she makes little effort and expects other children to come to assist her.

The concerns involved for transferring to secondary school

1 Her parents are concerned that too much will be expected of her in PE and that her interest in the subject will decline further.

2 Sally is worried that the new school will not understand her needs.

3 Both Sally and her parents are concerned that the teaching assistant will not be transferring to the secondary school and as yet no replacement has been found.

Advice for transferring from primary to secondary school

Many primary children have an opportunity to visit their new school in July, before transferring in September. This is particularly important for children who have sight problems and who may well require more than one visit, to take in their new surroundings. In order to increase Sally's confidence she spent some time familiarising herself with the various PE facilities at the school, such as the gym, pool and changing-rooms. She also looked at the routes between the sports facilities and the main part of the school.

The new support staff, as well as PE staff learnt about modifications and adjustments for pupils with impaired vision before Sally arrived. One of the PE staff made a visit to see Sally "in action" at her primary school to see her capabilities in a familiar environment. This gave the PE staff some idea of the assistance that would be needed, her skill level, and an understanding of "safety" rules that would need to be appropriately applied.

Sally's parents also had opportunities to discuss concerns that they had about PE with the Special Needs staff and the PE staff at the new school. Useful information was gained from the parents that helped to clarify the total picture.

It was agreed that in-service training for staff would be helpful and that it would be beneficial for Sally's new peer group to explore the practical and social implications of visual impairment, perhaps using the Personal, Social and Health Curriculum. A mutual exchange of knowledge and myths would enable Sally's peers to respond positively to her needs, and also help Sally to feel more confident about her transition to secondary school.

Athletics

Athletics is a great sport for both individual performance and team participation. It is a good sport for basic skill development, improving confidence and mobility. Young people who have sight problems can follow many different pathways; whether it is a fun introductory session, regular sports lessons, taking part in school sports days, or competing at inter-school competitions or national junior competitions for athletes with impaired vision.

Safety

There are some key safety issues to stress for a young person with a sight problem.

General safety rules for athletics should apply for all athletics sessions, including sessions specifically for young people with sight problems.

In addition it is important to check that the young person's eye condition or recent eye surgery does not prevent them from doing high impact events such as long jump or high jump, or sports involving heavy lifting. If in any doubt, ask the young person's parent to seek advice from their ophthalmologist.

Many young people wish to wear their glasses for sport, so that they can see as well as possible. Many children with sight problems feel very disoriented without their glasses on, and this has a huge effect on their confidence. When assessing any risk, it is important to consider the safety of all involved. Occasionally glasses might be damaged or broken, and whilst hugely inconvenient it is unlikely to injure anyone. If in doubt, seek advice from the young person's eye specialist.

Some people with sight problems are affected by bright sunlight. They may find it painful and the brightness or glare can mean they can see very little. Always check. Some athletes may wish to wear a peaked sun hat, or prescription tinted glasses. Some may prefer an indoor physical activity on a particularly bright day.

Wherever possible keep equipment in one location and not lying around where it could be a hazard.

Remember for throwing events that a young person with a sight problem needs another person to confirm that the throwing area is clear and that it is safe to throw. The sighted guide also needs to describe the outcome of the throw ie how far it went and in which direction. This information is vital to help young people with sight problems gradually understand the effect of their throwing actions, and to modify their technique to achieve better results.

Making it possible

It is important to orientate the young person around the area and point out any potential hazards. Start by enabling the young person to become confident in one area before introducing a safe route to the next. It takes more time and effort for a child with a sight problem to build up a mental picture of an area, as they are doing this sequentially small area by small area, and rarely have the immediate overall view that a sighted child gets on arrival. Remember to be descriptive when talking to all the participants - it is not helpful to point to an object or to say it is "over there"! Using everyone's name as often as possible also helps a young person with a sight problem to keep track of what is going on in the group.

A young person with a sight problem should be allowed to handle equipment to become familiar with it, before being taught how to use it.

Consider using brightly coloured equipment such as bibs or foam javelins. Think about colour tone contrasting equipment. It is also useful to ensure that any lane markings, jumping areas and throwing areas are clearly marked too, as this makes them a lot easier to see. Some children with sight problems need tactile markings, so that they can feel the edge of an area with their feet.

Running

Sighted children learn to run in a straight line relatively effortlessly. They receive constant visual feedback about their position in relation to other runners and the finishing line. Many children with sight problems need help to learn to run confidently. And some also benefit from a programme devised by a mobility specialist to develop confident movement and spatial understanding. Mobility specialists are employed either by the education authority or by social services. Parents can request mobility help for their children, or can ask the special needs coordinator at school or the specialist teacher for children with impaired vision to make a request on their behalf. Some children benefit from using a running machine at walking pace to learn to walk "naturally", swinging their arms as they walk.

© BBS

Young children with little vision can be encouraged to run towards a caller who is just six paces ahead of them. Gradually the distance can be lengthened as the child's confidence increases.

An older child might be encouraged to run 50m by having a caller standing at 25m and a second caller at the finishing line. Gradually these distances can be increased. A caller can simply repeatedly call the runner's name.

A more sophisticated calling system can be introduced on the athletics track. The runner with sight problems can start a run in lane five. Their caller repeatedly calls "5" while the runner remains in lane. The caller calls "4" if the runner veers to the left and "6" if the runner moves to the right. With practice this helps a runner with sight problems to follow the track. It is important that a runner with sight problems is given plenty of time to get used to the caller's voice.

In practice, in a race situation it is often helpful to allocate two lanes for a runner with sight problems, to give more leeway.

Whilst learning to run in lane is a useful skill, runners with sight problems almost always use a guide runner for competitions.

The sighted guide runs alongside the runner with sight problems. They each hold one end of a guide rope. The guide rope consists of two loops of rope covered in tape or fabric so that it is comfortable to hold and does not cause friction on the runners' hands. The rope in between the loops needs to be long enough that the guide runner can run in the lane next to the runner with sight problems, but short enough to feel each others' running movement - approximately 25cm - but you can adjust this to suit the runners.

It is important that the guide runs alongside, not ahead and not behind. In a competition the runner with sight problems would be disqualified if the guide runner were seen to be pulling, as this is unfair assistance! Towards the end of the race the guide runner can encourage the runner with sight problems to lead slightly.

The guide runner needs to be able to run comfortably at the pace set by the blind or partially sighted runner. The two runners need to build up a relationship of trust. They can start with jogging for a short distance on grass, and gradually grow accustomed to running together. Sometimes a young person with a sight problem may want to run alone, and aim to "beat" their previous times.

To include children with sight problems in relay races takes a little additional thought and more opportunities to practise. All children benefit from plenty of opportunities to practise baton exchanges. It can be helpful for a runner with sight problems to run 1st or 4th so that only one baton exchange is required. For younger children you may decide that a hand touch is acceptable rather than using batons.

To practise real baton exchanges it is best to try short distances initially, as synchronisation is not easy, and even top athletes experience poor changeovers on occasion.

Track events are a useful opportunity to help children develop a better understanding of distances. It can be useful to ask children to work out how many paces a particular distance is, or to walk the track using a clicking metre wheel. Talking stopwatches are also useful in helping children to appreciate achievements and to help them make estimates for the time a race might take over a particular distance.

For older children running machines may be used as an aid to improving stamina. However a thorough induction is needed and appropriate supervision to ensure safety both on and off the machine. For more on the use of fitness machines please see the multigym section on page 21.

Long jump

Young athletes with sight problems can start by doing a standing jump to get used to landing safely in the sandpit. Some participants need lots of clear description about bending knees for take-off and landing and learning to "fall forwards".

It is important to encourage young people with sight problems to be involved in the measuring of their jump, so that they can appreciate their own progress and put it in the context of others' achievements too. Being part of the process also helps them to develop a better understanding of distances, experiencing mathematics in a practical setting and to develop better spatial understanding. (See Equipment section for specialist measuring equipment on page 49.)

It is quite a challenge for a young person with sight problems to run up and jump from the usual take-off board. One approach is to make a chalked area on the runway in the metre before the take-off board. This can be made with chalk mixed with a small amount of sand. The young person can take-off anywhere in the chalked area, and the jump is measured from the take-off mark left in the chalk to the landing mark in the pit.

A long jumper who has a sight problem can also be assisted by up to two callers. One caller can be near the take-off area and help the athlete stay on course and tell the athlete when to jump. Another can call from the pit, again to help the athlete's sense of direction. (For more information about techniques for callers please see the Running section on page 16.)

High jump

High jump is considered a high impact sport, and is not suitable for children who have retinal problems or who have had recent eye surgery.

Children with sight problems need the opportunity to familiarise themselves with the high jump posts and bar. All children need reassurance that the bar will fall if knocked into, and some children want an individual demonstration for themselves. Children with sight problems may have had some nasty bumps in the past and it is quite natural to be reluctant to incur injury.

The bar and/or posts can be made more visible using yellow and black tape or paint. A caller can also be used to help a child know when to jump. It is really important for young people with sight problems to start with a low bar and to experience success, so that confidence can be built up.

Descriptions of the jumping techniques need to be very specific, and it is good practice to ask the young person to explain in their own words what actions are expected, as this helps to clarify what has been understood. Some children may wish to start with a standing jump, as coordinating the run up to the bar is an additional set of complex skills to learn. (Please see the Long jump section for more on running approaches on page 17.)

Again, it is good practice to talk to children about the height of the bar, discuss where it comes up to on their body, and remind them of their progress.

For children who are wheelchair users an alternative to high jump is a game called "Height Bean Bag". Children take turns to throw beanbags over the bar and are allowed three attempts. This is a good activity for encouraging arm extension and throwing skills.

Field events

Javelin

When introducing young people to throwing javelins it is important that all participants have understood and respect the safety instructions. A sighted partner should always confirm that the throwing area is clear before a throw takes place, and that no one is behind the thrower. It can be useful to give participants an opportunity to inspect or feel the hole that a javelin leaves in the ground to help them to appreciate the power of the impact of a javelin.

© Linda Fisher

© BBS

It is important to start by practising standing throws, so that a young person can focus on their throwing technique, before introducing the more demanding co-ordination required of a run up and throw. (For more on run ups and the use of callers please see the Long jump section on page 17.)

Alternatives to traditional javelins are available. Brightly coloured foam javelins can be useful to develop throwing techniques and these can also be used in a sports hall.

Turbo javelins are plastic but weighted, which allows participants to see or feel that the ground is marked on landing.

Young people with sight problems should take part in measuring the length of throw to help them to develop their understanding of distances, and to appreciate improvements in their own performance, and that of their peers.

Shot put and discus

For all throwing events it is essential that all participants have understood and respect the safety instructions. A sighted partner should always confirm that the throwing area is clear before a throw takes place, and the area around the thrower should be clear in case the throw does not go in the intended direction. Participants need to appreciate that heavy projectiles can cause very severe injury if they were to hit a person.

It is important to demonstrate warm up exercises very clearly so that young people with sight problems learn to warm up correctly. Very clear language is needed to teach correct body movements and throwing and releasing techniques. It may be necessary to move the children's limbs through the appropriate throwing actions. Before doing so, you must ask the child's permission each time.

Some participants might find it helpful to develop appropriate techniques with a lighter weight object. For shot put a group could start with ball throwing competitions, before being introduced to a real shot.

Young people with sight problems should take part in measuring the length of throw. It is valuable for them to develop their understanding of distances, and to appreciate improvements in their own performance, and that of their peers.

What can be achieved?

Athletics gives all participants an opportunity to learn more about different types of physical activity and to discover their preferences and strengths, and to build on their current level of fitness. Taking part in school athletics may encourage some young people to join an athletics club and get regular coaching in order to improve their level of skill, fitness and performance.

British Blind Sport runs annual national junior and senior athletics championships as well as squad training sessions that develop and encourage young athletes who have a sight problem. There is the potential to compete nationally at junior or senior level, as well as opportunities at international and paralympic level too.

On the whole athletes with sight problems participate and compete in the same events as mainstream athletes do, although as yet there are no formal competitions for athletes with sight problems doing hurdles, hammer, pole vault and steeplechase.

Alan Whetherley
Development Officer for Visually Impaired People
London Sports Forum for Disabled People

Using multigyms

Increasingly gyms based in leisure and fitness centres are offering sessions for young people, and many secondary schools are investing in fitness suites. The use of such facilities is a useful option to explore for a young person with a sight problem, who may wish to increase their personal fitness but struggles with taking part in fast moving team games timetabled for school physical education lessons.

Many gyms have lower age limits in order to ensure that young people are physically and emotionally mature enough to use the machines safely and responsibly. All young people should have an individual induction plan, and a programme devised by a qualified fitness instructor to meet their individual needs and level of fitness. The fitness programme needs to include a personal warm up routine. A young person with a sight problem requires a careful introduction to each piece of equipment, and lots of time to become familiar with the layout of the room. All routes around the gym hall must be kept clear of obstructions at all times. In particular weights should never be left lying around.

When using a running machine for the first time a young person with a sight problem may wish to begin at a walking pace and to hold the sides initially. As users' confidence increases they can let go and begin to vary the speed and resistance settings.

The lottery-funded "Inclusive Fitness Initiative" can provide information about equipment designed to be accessible to users with a wide variety of needs including sight problems. These include large, bright and/or raised displays that can be read by a user with a sight problem and well thought out contrasting colour schemes and adjustable features to enable users to use the machines and receive performance feedback independently. Information about accessible fitness facilities around the country, inclusively designed machines and suppliers is available from www.inclusivefitness.org

Alan Whetherley
Development Officer for Visually Impaired People
London Sports Forum for Disabled People

Dance and gymnastics

Benefits of dance and gymnastics

Dance and creative gymnastic movement is a visual art. It has no finish line, winning time or distance and no match score to measure its success. It supports use of language, numeracy, humanities and environmental awareness. It offers reinforcement to balance, co-ordination, locomotion, mobility skills and enhances personal and social skills.

Its success is subjective and for the performer is measured in their solo or group satisfaction and the pleasure shown by any observers. Most children who have sight problems love to dance, rhythms excite them and they welcome the freedom in travelling, of using a large space, floor and air, in a way that uses their imagination and extends their bodies in a non-competitive setting. Creative gymnastics shares similar elements with the addition of "landmarks", mats, small and large pieces of apparatus. There is a freedom of choice in how to answer a movement task, sequence different movements and arrive at a satisfying conclusion.

The challenge

It is this very freedom that makes creative movement a challenge to teach and structure, to enable a child who has sight problems to develop their movement vocabulary to its optimum. The working area must be safe with sufficient space and non-slip surfaces. Barefoot work should be encouraged, and adult support and supervision of others in the group are paramount to building the child's confidence in these experiences.

Children who are partially sighted may benefit from a close up demonstration of what is required. For a child who has no sight experience of their extended environment, and who has difficulty in reproducing a movement by imitation, traditional demonstration should be replaced with clear uncluttered explanation. The teacher's choice of descriptive words should "paint a picture in the mind's eye."

For example, it is not enough to ask a child to lift their knee; how high should they lift it, in which direction should it point, is the leg straight or bent and should the foot be pointed or flat?

What does a pointed foot look like and why does it look better for this or that movement sequence?

The supporting adult is key to making that transfer from what the child is "feeling" to how the shape or movement is "looking", rather like providing a language translation. The child with sight problems may have a fixed "point of view," unable to evaluate from a change of position unless they have the benefit of visual memory prior to their sight loss.

Time spent helping children to get to know their body mechanics builds their confidence rapidly; children learn the physical proximity of one body part to another, the differences between large and small body areas and learn how to manage the transfer of weight from one to another with ease.

The coach's role in these lessons is to reinforce the development of motor skills through the more effective use of sensory skills. The development of concepts such as their "midline," the discrimination of size and shape and how to organise a route or pathway, are fundamental but sometimes far from obvious to a child with sight problems, and these concepts need to be taught overtly.

A visual impairment, whether total or partial can reduce a child's opportunities to experiment, which may result in an underdeveloped body image and diminished drive to explore the use of space. Indeed some children with sight problems have a fear of exploring space, particularly if they have had more than their fair share of bumps and scrapes from walking into or tripping over things.

Making a start

It is useful to find out whether the child or young person has taken part in any mobility and orientation education (sometimes called mobility training). You may be able to talk to the mobility teacher to find out more about the child's existing skills and knowledge. If a child hasn't received any mobility education it can be worth raising their need for this with parents and the child's school. If children are unable to orientate without key landmarks it can heighten their anxiety.

The key is to make experimenting with space and position fun. One way to start is by handling different shaped objects: a ball, mat roll, a fan, a spoked-wheel and then move into copying the shape, moving into and away from their "centre".

This is non-threatening but is already encouraging them to explore to the outer limits of their personal space. Each should be described by the movement words, building the shapes vocabulary - rounded, tucked, stretched, narrow, wide. They begin to enjoy moving away from their "centre" safely and in this way mental mapping begins to function and develop into a set of strategies for moving safely through the space around them.

The element of adventurous body management is not obvious to a child who has sight problems; they tend always to operate in their "safe zone" naturally. The mechanics of experimenting with moving from adjacent body parts to others that are separated by distance, make an easy transition into movement words and actions such as "rolling", "stepping", "jumping", "hopping", "striding", "balancing" and "stillness". A sequence can be created easily from these starter movements with stillness and preparation, followed by the execution of a task, completed by stillness in a balance to finish.

"Forward or backward chaining" of selected movements is helpful to all children. It not only teaches them to create a transition or link from one part of a sequence to another, but also reinforces movement memory for what has gone before and what comes next.

The changes of level in their own body shape, parts that are high, medium or low level, can be translated into exploring the different levels in their personal space.

Example activity

"Can you draw a circle with your elbow high beside your head, then beside your hip and low beside your foot?"

"Now can you link those three circle movements together into one continuous movement and then pass the movement over to your other elbow?"

This exercise and others like it can introduce the idea that in their personal or extended space, different body parts can work at any of the three levels, in front of them, to the sides, behind them, above and below them. A movement pattern is building in their "mind's eye" as a movement memory. Can it be repeated accurately? Could it then be repeated with a change added such as tracing one circle quicker than the others and one circle slower, or enlarge the size of one circle.

Using objects to illustrate spatial concepts

It is helpful to use concrete objects to illustrate spatial concepts. For example, you can assist a child to stand in the centre of a doorway and stretch to feel the top corners and the lower corners, using a chair or bench if necessary. Set a movement task of using a chosen body part such as an elbow or hand to stretch towards the corners of the doorway into a continuous movement, then re-visit two opposite corners before finishing. Now invite the young person to step out of the doorway and copy that same movement sequence from memory. A sighted partner could copy, mirror or stretch in opposite directions to the partner who has sight

problems, working towards and away from their centre.

Similarly, use a table top to "feel spaces" in front, to the sides and behind, turning or orientating towards or away from the table.

A wheel that spins freely on its hub, or a maths "click-wheel", can illustrate the third plane of movement. Attach a piece of tactile tape or tie a string to a point around the wheel edge. Now help the child to maintain hand contact with it to feel it move around to return to the start of the circle. This concept can then be experienced by carrying movements from standing on the floor to sitting, rolling onto their back to lift feet in the air above their head, allowing the momentum to rock back to sitting and return to standing. These movements enable young people to "feel" the air space in this plane. Arms stretched in front, down towards the floor, then out forwards and upwards help in tracing a similar aerial pathway. Children can use wand-mounted ribbons and flags to create these three-plane sequences. The wands and flags are tactile and create great sounds as they whirl through the air around the three dimensions.

Creating a safe working area

An elastic circle can be used to provide a space with boundaries. This space limiter can be either for safety in a large class or for children with very poor spatial awareness. This is simply a circle of elastic (covered with fabric for comfort) as large as you choose for a group, or smaller circles for individuals. With other members of the group outside maintaining the shape, an individual or partners can work inside. In this way the elastic and its enclosed space connects everyone to the task, as each takes their turn.

This is an ideal introduction to creating routes and pathways building a mental map of shape, direction and orientation. Other children in the group, apparatus or objects placed within the working area can become landmarks. When a pathway has been created it could be replicated by a model such as a rope on the floor or a tactile diagram on paper, to assist a child who has a sight problem to evaluate it.

Experiencing changes in body shape and direction

Children also have great fun with "body bags," which allow them to physically feel changes of body shape and direction such as twists and spirals. These are made of lightweight stretch material the shape of a tea-bag large enough to allow a child to stand and stretch fully inside, with zips on the "shoulders". Made in bright colours, children who are partially sighted enjoy using these bags working in pairs, copying, mirroring, meeting and parting, moving over, under and around a partner. Equally the children who are blind enjoy feeling the connection the bag allows between locating different body parts simultaneously, improving their perceived body image.

As a child's body management and spatial awareness skills develop, they increasingly enjoy moving with others. It is important that they do work in harmony or to complement others and not in isolation.

Total or acquired blindness in children require adjustments to be made in a movement class and answering a movement task with other children may require more use of touch. Use a touch exercise, where one child passes a movement cue by touch to another child, each using a chosen body part, such as head, elbow, knee or foot. This requires everyone to be in close proximity and can be like a game of statues, each moving and freezing in turn. Close adult support in such an exercise is important.

It is important to find out at what distance a child can see clearly and whether they can see above and below, to left and right without turning their head. Some children may have reduced depth perception, meaning that stairs might appear to them more like a flat zebra crossing, and the edge of a mat may just seem like a change of colour of the floor. Where possible it is good to encourage children to use the vision they have.

Performing in a sighted group

More advanced pupils have enjoyed involvement in dance projects in the wider community with sighted pupils from other colleges and schools. This annual county based project has involved work with professional dancers/teachers, has provided extension opportunities and a sense of pride for the young people in participating in a choreographed group performance piece. Rehearsal-support from an adult with specialist knowledge concerning lighting, optimum visual positioning and "coaching" between rehearsals, using forward and backward chaining techniques, were instrumental in the success of the dancers who have sight problems. This was also a source of pride for the organisers that such a large visual project could be successfully inclusive.

When successful, movement work is fun, should always be safe and builds immense self-esteem.

Dance ideas

Tap out rhythm clapping, stamping, on body, on floor, on instrument.

Look at exercises and routines with physiotherapy exercise balls, solo use of wand ribbons and flags for dance.

Dance in-touch and contact, to mirror partner work or as a movement cue, rhythm on partner's body with partner movement reply.

Use hoops for gym and dance, for spatial extensions, inside, outside, around, above, below, under, over, midline, left and right.

Similarly, the group "giant elastic circle" for dance or gym floor-work, provides a safe area to experiment with pathways and routes, and encourages working with others in their group. It is extremely important that a child with sight problems is fully included in the work, and feels valued as a member of the group.

© Jill Clark

Using "body bags" for dance to "feel" shape under tension, enables different body parts to work in opposition simultaneously.

© Jill Clark

Movement with shakers, bells, tambourines and drums, wood blocks or rhythm sticks to carnival, samba, steel band or "Stomp!-type" music.

Using a wide range of audio stimuli such as music, voices, stories, poems, sound effects and child-led tapped rhythms is beneficial to all members of a group. You can offer a wide range of motivators and using sound is an excellent aid to location and orientation.

Sound cues can be used to signal changes of level or direction.

Wearing wrist or ankle band bells alerts other children when travelling.

Ropes, group elastic band, chalked pathways, long pieces of material, brightly coloured rubber spots and arrows are all useful for routing.

Changes of floor surface can be used as foot cues to a change of movement or pathway.

Gymnastics

Walking along a bench is a frightening task for a child who has a sight loss. Give the child time to hand-explore the surface. Let them stand next to it to work out its height in relation to their own body. Let them work out its length, sit on it, kneel on it before finally standing on it with your support.

Allow the child to place an open hand on your shoulder for support - they can often take a fearful vice-like grip on an offered hand.

Support under the child's elbows or at the side of hips when they are confident enough to take the lead, encourages good posture or chosen body shape.

Encourage a wide movement vocabulary in floor work before introducing large pieces of apparatus. At a later stage, select part of a floor routine and use it to approach or leave the apparatus piece.

Large crash mats or a soft play area is a safer setting for a child to experiment with new body management or spatial tasks.

© Jill Clark

The use of background music may offer a child who has sight problems cues or timing through a sequence of movement tasks.

Use this discreetly in a chosen area to avoid disturbance to other children's work. Alternatively use the music for everyone in the group.

Plan a gymnastic journey, over, under, through, around, swing, jump, stretch, balance and roll. Use movement words with clear explanation. Make a tactile route diagram.

Give time to experiment with more than one way to answer the action task, so that the child is encouraged to evaluate and discover that choices can be made.

If working in or through an apparatus space, allow the child time to examine it for dimension and height, and angle of entry or exit.

As a sighted child mentally rehearses a movement task before executing it, a dancer or gymnast with sight problems requires time to mentally "forward chain" their movement plan.

Teach safe landing from an early stage using a variety of levels and from different apparatus, always in a well padded area.

Encourage barefoot work, it reinforces good balance and poise, strengthens muscles and maintains suppleness in foot, ankle and knee.

Formal gymnastics

For a child who enjoys their gymnastic work at school, joining a gymnastics club can be a very positive step. A club that welcomes children of all abilities can play a key role in helping a gymnast with a sight problem to reach their full potential. It is essential that a club can offer a one-to-one coach or observer for a child with sight problems as the standard demonstration to a large group is ineffective. At the same time it is important that the gymnast with a sight problem is safe and part of their working group, and is socially included. It is vital that the coaches are informed about children's level of vision and any implications their eye condition may have for gymnastics. For example, children at risk of retinal detachment should not undertake high impact landings.

Achieving personal excellence

Excellence of performance is the basis for judgements in a gymnastics club setting and most clubs divide the young people into defined groups according to ability; those who make up the more advanced squad and those who form the "recreation" groups. Gymnasts often work towards award schemes. It is important for a gymnast with a sight problem to understand that groups are based on ability and not age. A sight impairment can mean it takes longer to develop certain skills, purely because sighted children have the advantage of watching the movements of others, which helps to reinforce their own work. In a large club, all children progress at different rates and age need not be an issue. Good clubs encourage young people to consider their own progress over time, rather than focusing on the rate of progress of others.

Orientation

Most gymnastic halls will have some static pieces of equipment that remain in the same place each session, such as the asymmetric bars, a pit, a tumble strip. Other items will come and go depending on the activities and circuits for that particular session. It is vital that a gymnast is given the opportunity each session to orientate themselves and to gain a mental map of the position of apparatus. Likewise when apparatus is adjusted to suit a gymnast's skill level or physique, a gymnast with a sight problem needs to be fully informed, often needing the opportunity to feel the new height of a vault, bar or beam. Every movement task will be sequentially learnt and approaches to apparatus need support from the coach in "back and forward chaining" to help the gymnast judge distance, speed, timing and body position changes.

The trampoline is often used as a teaching aid and helps a gymnast with a sight problem to build their movement memory in flight. Using the trampoline offers the gymnast and the coach space and time to make adjustments, to repeat specific elements of a sequence without the need to negotiate around additional pieces of apparatus or other gymnasts. Trampolining involves high impact landings. Coaches must check whether this is safe for the young persons' eye condition.

Floorwork

The gymnast needs to scan and pace the mat area to appreciate the size of the floor area available to work in. Coaches can help gymnasts with a commentary on speed and when to start a round-off or a tumble sequence in order to stay within the designated floor area.

Feedback with regard to direction can also be helpful where gymnasts are doing half or full turn spins. Tape on the mat can also be helpful to enable a gymnast to place his or her hands in a straight line for a perfect cartwheel.

Vault

Many young people with sight problems find it difficult to coordinate the judgement of closing distance, body space and apparatus, and will struggle to execute a run-up to a vault with speed and accuracy.

It is vital to backchain the approach into the take-off element. Counting and using verbal cues are helpful, such as "lift", "jump" or "push".

The approach strip and the vault itself can be made more visible using brightly coloured markers, such as vinyl throw downs or tape.

Asymmetric bars

All gymnasts begin with the lower of the two bars and need to reach quite a level of proficiency before moving on to the higher bar. Gymnasts who have very little or no sight may be disoriented by the introduction of the higher bar and experience difficulty in judging the distance between bars. Every gymnast is an individual.

Balance beam

A beam that contrasts well in colour to the floor colour will be easier for children with some vision to see. When gymnasts progress to routines that require precise "spotting" it can be difficult for a child with a sight problem to judge their position. Some children find it helpful if the end of the beam is marked with bright paint or tape.

Parallel bars

For male gymnasts who have some sight it is important to make the bars as visible as possible, using tape or paint. It is for coaches to judge whether an individual gymnast will be safe to attempt a movement that involves landing back onto arms support in flight.

Setting targets

For all children it is best to set achievable goals and to encourage the gymnast to achieve them to a high standard. Setting realistic goals helps to boost a child's confidence and sense of achievement as well as reducing the chance of injury. The British Gymnastics Association organises regional and national competitions for children with disabilities and good coaches will welcome this additional dimension to their club.

Jill Clark
Head of Physical Education
West of England School, Exeter

Football

Football holds the same fascination for people who have sight problems as it does for everyone else. Some of the players who play for their country in the England Blind Football Team lost their sight in accidents, but many were born blind and have never had the opportunity to see a football. They have never seen the all time greats - Pele, Beckham, Best, and yet they still play the game with the same passion and wonderful skill.

Many sighted people are intrigued by football for people with sight problems. It is a mistake to think that because the players have sight loss, the game is less physical. Most think it is a dangerous sport, but this notion soon fades when they witness a correctly organised match. Despite the heavy collisions that go on, there are surprisingly few serious injuries.

Why include children with sight problems?

Football plays a high profile role in school life. Physical education lessons for both boys and girls frequently include football skills, football is often played in the playground and many schools participate in football matches with neighbouring schools. In addition, thousands of children and young people take part in football training and matches at weekends. Football is a popular spectator sport in Britain and many people enjoy watching matches and commenting on the changing fortunes of local and national teams.

Including children and young people with sight problems in football, not only enables them to develop fitness skills, it also gives them an opportunity to be included in one of the interests shared by many other children and adults.

Creating a good atmosphere to promote learning

In order to motivate players successfully, the football coach needs to take into consideration the following factors:

1   Enthusiasm can often make up for lack of skill

2   Communication and concentration skills are essential for a player with a sight problem

3   Mobility and spatial awareness skills have to be developed and worked on.

Session 1 - mobility and movement

Football requires players not only to run but also to stop, start and change direction with or without the ball. These are the most important aspects to consider when coaching someone who has a sight problem. Coaching correct techniques in mobility and movement minimises risk of injury to players and others. Significant time should be spent developing these skills before a player participates in a competitive game.

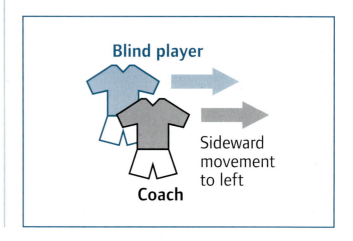

Blind player

Sideward movement to left

Coach

1 The player stands behind the coach with hands on the coach's shoulders. (The player must be arm's length away from the coach).

2 Both the player and the coach must stand up on their toes with feet shoulder width apart. The coach instructs the player to follow his or her movement. For example, if the coach makes a right sideward movement, the player must follow. The object of this exercise is for the player to pick up a sense of rhythm from the coach.

3 In order to be sure that instructions have been understood, the coach should then reverse the roles. This way, the coach can observe and correct the situation if necessary.

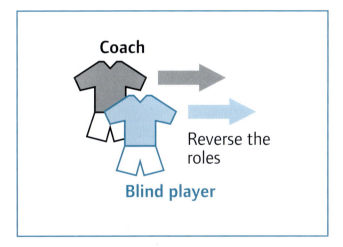

Coach

Reverse the roles

Blind player

Session 2 - sideward movements

This is the same exercise as above, but this time the player stands on his or her own.

1 Check the player's stance.

2 Instruct the player to move sideways to the left and then the right using quick steps.

3 Once the exercise has been mastered, the player's speed should be increased.

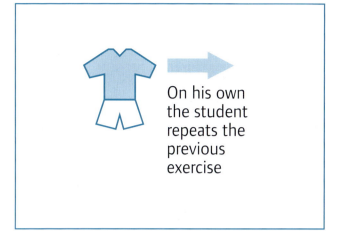

On his own the student repeats the previous exercise

4 You can call various directions to the player, ie quick to the left, back to the right etc. This should be continued until the player feels confident and is moving smoothly.

5 The player can then progress to moving forwards and backwards two or three metres. This can be achieved by the coach working alongside the player, ie working side by side.

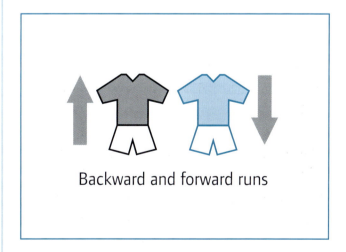

Backward and forward runs

Session 3 – introduce the football

These exercises teach the player to react by listening for the sound of the ball (the ball has a bell in it, or ball bearings or lead shot). (See Equipment list for suppliers of audible footballs on pages 47-48).

1 Player stands in starting position ie on toes. The coach stands two or three metres away and rolls the ball at the player. The player reacts by rolling the ball back to the coach.

2 The coach can then roll the ball to the side of the player, and coach the player using clear directional language to move his or her body in the path of the line of the ball.

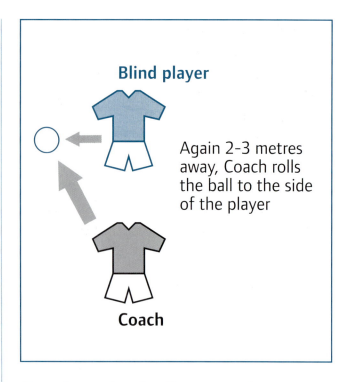

Again 2-3 metres away, Coach rolls the ball to the side of the player

Session 4 – ball control with the inside of the foot

1 The player should be up in the starting position ie on toes. The coach should explain and show the player what part of the foot to use.

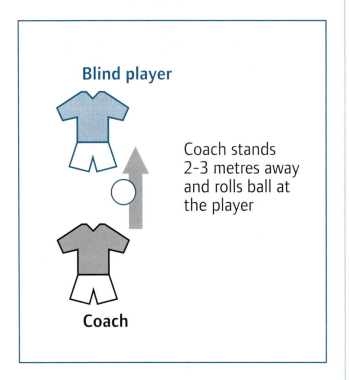

Coach stands 2-3 metres away and rolls ball at the player

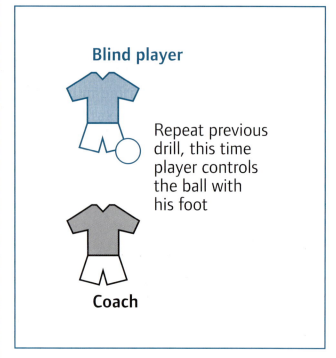

Repeat previous drill, this time player controls the ball with his foot

3 Once the player has improved, the coach can roll the ball more quickly to the player and eventually introduce the player to controlling the ball with the side of the foot and with the sole.

2 Stand three metres away and roll the ball directly towards the player. The player listens to the ball and presents the inside of the foot. Then the player can roll the ball back. Once a player has gained confidence and can control the ball successful when rolled directly towards him or her you can progress to the procedures outlined in Session 3 ie rolling the ball to either side of the player.

Coaching children who have little sight or are blind is obviously complex, but with a little thought and effort, football skills can be developed and the game enjoyed. The above exercises are merely an introduction to what can be achieved.

Including a player with sight problems in matches

It is the coach's responsibility to choose a football that is as visible and/or audible as possible. Find out from the player with sight problems if particular colours are easier for them to see, and think about making the ball colour contrast with the colour of the playing surface. The surface can make quite a difference to the sound of a ball.

Introducing and explaining rules

Not all children will be familiar with the finer points of the rules so it is useful for the whole group to discuss the rules before a match. Keep it simple, and use clear descriptive language and demonstrations. For beginners, use small teams, playing on a small area. Use brightly coloured bibs and ask the players to keep in touch verbally to help the team mate who has a sight problem locate them. Where a child has some vision make the goals more visible using contrasting tapes such as yellow and black. It also helps to make pitch markings as visible as possible. Ask the player what helps. (See Equipment list for information about vinyl markings on page 48.)

© Alan Whetherley

When the game begins it can be helpful to have an ongoing commentary from a support worker or coach. The referee can also be asked to explain decisions more fully than by giving the usual hand signals, so that a child with a sight problem understands what is going on and why.

Encouraging team play

Some coaches use scoring strategies to encourage other team members to pass to particular players. For example, if the boys in a mixed team are "hogging" the ball a coach may decide that a goal scored by a girl scores two points and one by a boy is only worth one. Obviously the reverse can be true! Such strategies however need to be considered carefully and introduced with sensitivity.

Competitive football for blind and partially sighted players

Blind and partially sighted football has been played in this country for more than 25 years. The game requires equal measures of aural dexterity and twinkle-toed skills. Using a football containing ball bearings that rattle loudly, players track the movements of the opposition by the sound of their feet. This emphasis on sound means that spectators are respectfully asked to remain silent during games, but advice is offered by the respective coaches from behind the goals.

Games are played on pitches roughly the size of a five-a-side pitch and teams consist of four outfield players, all of whom are blind or partially sighted, and one sighted keeper. The goals are similar in size to those used in hockey.

Due to slightly differing levels of blindness, all players competing in the B1 (totally blind category) wear eye patches and soft shades to ensure that no one is able to gain any advantage using light perception, however slight. Using their highly tuned spatial awareness, the sound of the ball and the players around them, the teams are able to play a game very similar in pace and intensity to the football played by fully sighted footballers. In addition, the team's eyes are the coaching staff, one of whom patrols the halfway line and one of whom calls the players in from behind the opposition's goal.

Tony Larkin - Sport and Recreation Programme Coordinator Royal National College for the Blind

Tony Larkin is an ex-professional footballer of 16 years and has been the England Team Manager since 1995 for the B1 totally blind football team and the B2 and B3 partially sighted football squad. Through his work at the Royal National College for the Blind in Hereford he has been involved with football for people with visual impairment for over 15 years. He has taken the B1 football teams to three World Championships.

(This chapter is based upon an article which first appeared in RNIB's education magazine Visability, Spring 2003.)

Goalball

What is goalball?

Goalball is a three-a-side game developed for players who have sight problems. The great thing about goalball is that sighted people can join in as everyone wears blacked out goggles. Goalball has three main features that distinguish it from games played by sighted people:

1 All players wear blacked out goggles, knee and elbow pads which ensure that everyone plays on an even and equal level.

2 The ball used contains an internal bell that enables the player to hear and locate it on the court during play.

3 The game is played on a volleyball (or similar size court) with tactile markings. All the string tactile markings on the court are taped down so that players can feel their position.

When players hear the ball coming towards their end of the court, they dive towards the ball to block it with their body. A goal is scored if it goes past the back line of the court.

Goalball can be played at both recreational and competitive level. There are competitons and leagues arranged for teams new to the game (development) and for more advanced players (experienced). There is a Great Britain Goalball team, and regular squad training sessions are held too.

There is a "Goalball Leaders" course which would enable a teacher/volunteer to learn about the game, how to mark out the court and basic skill development. For those who are ambitious there is a "Goalball Referee" course too.

Goalball has an excellent website where you can access up-to-date information on the game and forthcoming events. See www.goalball.co.uk

Alan Whetherley
Development Officer for Visually
Impaired People
London Sports Forum for Disabled
People

© Leicester Mercury

Judo

■ Case study

"I am the only kid in my judo class who can't see but I still love it."

The above quote was taken from a letter from Kate, an eight year old girl who is registered blind.

Kate first became interested in judo at the age of 6 but was not aware of the facilities we had to offer. Kate came to us through Sports Vision, organised by a local group to give children with sight problems a chance at sport. She came along to one of our classes at the George H Carnall Centre in Manchester, which is the training ground for the Great Britain Visually Impaired Judo Squad.

Kate was a very shy girl, unsure of her potential and wary of her surroundings. We took her onto the mat and ran her around the perimeter to give her a feel for the scale of things. We showed her how to fall down safely, (break fall), so as not to injure herself. We introduced her to other players with sight problems and sighted players and took pleasure in her courage and enthusiasm. She enjoyed it so much that she now comes every Wednesday and now that her school has a lunch hour lesson she has the chance to practise every Thursday as well.

Kate has found a sport that she can play with other children whether sighted or not, and she doesn't need any special equipment.

Background

One of the rules of judo is that players must always hold on to their partner, and of course because each player has physical contact with the other, sight is not a prime requisite. Judo is an Olympic Sport which was developed over 120 years ago by a Japanese Professor called Jigoro Kano. He took the principles of Ju Jitsu and other martial arts, refined them by removing all the dangerous elements and added discipline, technique, and perfection, enabling players to compete without causing each other harm. The playing area (judo is a sport that is played - it is not about fighting) is made up of a compound rubber mat, which is used to cushion the fall. Each player takes hold of their partner and attempts to execute a particular move with the intention of throwing their partner to gain a win. The sport itself is likened to a physical game of chess, where each player attempts a "move", to which their partner counters and attacks and so on, until one player has the upper hand through technique and skill, and wins the throw.

Coaching a player with a sight problem

In order to teach judo, coaches need to understand how individual children relate to their environment, and put in place a training regime. Children and young people who have a sight problem benefit from one to one contact during the visual parts of class instruction, and quite often a sighted coach "patterns" the player through the moves, alongside the verbal instruction of the Class Coach. All players are always under the close supervision of the coaches, not only to further their judo skills, but also to ensure safety on the mat.

Because of the nature of the sport and the training provided, it has been proven that judo can enhance mind and body co-ordination enabling positive and faster reaction to problem solving and real life situations. Judo players also believe that it is judo, and not swimming, as is popularly thought, which best develops and exercises the muscles in the body.

Competitive judo

Great Britain has a Visually Impaired National Squad that competes around the world in major tournaments. The British team has been a top contender for a number of years with up and coming

youngsters like Ben Quilter who achieved international status at the age of 15 and is winning medals at every event.

Help for judo coaches

A full complement of trained BJA National Coaches in Manchester are dedicated to teaching judo to people with sight problems. This team is headed up by Steve Pullen, MBE 6th DAN and Clare Lynch, former chair of the British Blind Sports Judo Committee. The coaches are backed by the British Judo Association which is the National Governing Body for Judo in Britain, and supported by DOJO (the Disabled Open Judo Organisation), which is an organisation dedicated to helping and developing judo in areas of special needs.

Coaching seminars and training sessions for coaches are being developed, with a view to increasing our wealth of expertise in order to offer improved facilities for Special Needs Judo in the community. If you have a child who is interested in judo, if you are a teacher, or if you run a club and would like more information please contact the author or organisations listed on page 51.

Peter Topping 1st DAN
Coach for the Visually Impaired

This chapter is based upon an article, "Judo - the ideal sport for visually impaired children" which was first published in RNIB's education magazine Visability, Spring 2003.

Swimming

© Nigel Madhoo

Swimming is a great sport for all round physical fitness and wellbeing.

Being able to swim and being confident in water opens up many other water sport opportunities as well.

Early advice

As for any young child it is important for a child with a sight problem to play with water in the bath. They can play with toy boats and learn how things float and sink, get used to splashing water in their face, feel the water being swilled around them and try to do it themselves. In this way they begin to understand the nature of water and it is part of their lives from an early age.

From these early beginnings children can move on to paddling, taking part with a trusted adult in parent and baby classes just like any toddler might. They need to start to understand the many properties of water; the fact that it can be poured, it takes on the shape of a container, objects can float on it, information about depth, currents and waves. These properties take time to comprehend even for the toddlers with sight. But the many properties of water need to be experienced, explained and demonstrated to children who have a sight problem so that their understanding grows - remember they do not have the reinforcement of seeing water around them in its many forms.

A helper or teacher who is intending to take a youngster with a sight problem swimming, needs to be aware that the child may not have had as much experience of playing with water and understanding even basic facts about how water behaves. It will be important for the helper to fill in any gaps in children's experience or understanding as part of teaching them to swim.

Safety

Check with parents whether a child's eye condition limits any swimming activities. For example, some children with retinal problems may be advised against high impact activities such as diving, or jumping in. Children who have recently had eye surgery should be cleared by the doctor before going swimming.

It is not advisable to wear contact lenses in the pool, as the chances of losing them are too great, and being able to put your face in the water is essential for learning to swim correctly. Children who wear glasses or contact lenses may benefit from wearing prescription goggles in the pool. This enables them to make the best use of their vision in the swimming pool and to find their way to and from the changing rooms. Wearing goggles is preferable to glasses, which may come off in the water. If a child wears a prosthesis (artificial eye) this can be worn in the water providing that it fits well. However occasionally a prosthetic eye can come out at inconvenient moments, and if a pupil is likely to feel embarrassed when the coach has to dive in for it, it might be better to swim without it. If there is any likelihood that a prosthetic eye will come out it should not be worn for any water sports.

Make sure that children with sight problems understand and respect the rules of the swimming pool, as they may need help in reading wall signs concerning safety.

Beginner

Young children with sight problems can benefit from visiting the pool and changing rooms prior to their first lesson in peace and quiet. The noises are strange and echoing - they may love them and experiment with making their own noises, or they may hate them. It is useful to decide and talk through with the child who will help them, both on the way to the lesson and during the lesson. It can be useful on this first early visit to meet their helper, and begin to establish an early routine. It also enables the child to get used to their voice in this situation.

As in learning any new physical skill it is important that the early stages are taken slowly to build up confidence. Then it is important to repeat the skill in order to gain familiarity. Most things asked of the class should be reasonable to ask of a child with a sight problem who may just require a little further explanation from their helper. The helper should be reasonably confident in the water themselves. They

can then help to build confidence in the child, praising progress however small.

A small group is beneficial but not essential. Many children will come with their whole school class for swimming lessons in school time. Alternatively a child with a sight problem may be part of after school swimming lessons or an intensive course in the school holidays. In many swimming classes children take their turn and this waiting time gives the helper the time needed for extra explanation and it also gives time to talk about how the others in the class are progressing. It is helpful to the child with a sight problem to know that others will not necessarily achieve a new skill in the first lesson. In other words that children all learn skills at different rates and that other sighted children do not achieve instantly.

Improver

To improve a child's stroke takes patience and understanding of stroke technique. Observing a good swimmer in the class gives you a picture of how a good basic stroke is performed. Then ask yourself what is different about the stroke performed by the child who needs to improve and what therefore needs to be changed. It is important to concentrate on only one thing at a time. It is the same for learning any physical skill, one part at a time needs to be considered and reviewed before progressing to the next step.

Many of the basic practices used in any swimming lesson can help a child with a sight problem but be prepared to take time to fully explain what is required. Remember that many children with sight problems do not receive the constant reinforcement that sighted children do of seeing their peers perform something correctly. As children improve they grow in confidence and are then ready to move on to the next step.

It is important that children are given feedback to know they are improving and when they get a skill right. Much may depend on the helper being able to enthuse the child. Let them know how much further they have swum this week compared with last time, how much more smoothly they are moving, how many strokes they take to swim a width, how long they held their breath for, how they are doing compared with others. Be prepared to laugh with them and help them when things go astray and to applaud when there is progress.

A helper may either be in the water or helping from the poolside; if not maybe a buddy system could be used in the class. It depends on what the pupil would prefer. Having lanes roped off helps and encourages the young person to swim in a straight line. A caller in the water can also help the child's sense of direction.

Helping children to make friends with water

Any child who does not know how to swim can feel uncomfortable about saying so, particularly if they know friends who can swim. A child with sight problems who cannot swim is even more likely to think that he or she is the only one in a group that cannot swim as they do not always realise that others in the group are still beginners too.

Occasionally, for fear of embarrassment a child will not say they cannot swim, so it is important that the coach assesses all the children in the group at the first session. It helps the whole group if the coach makes it clear to all the children that they are all at different stages and that those who ask for help will get it.

Demonstrations

A child with a sight problem may not see a demonstration clearly enough but might not wish to draw attention to their sight problem and so says nothing. It is the coach's responsibility to make sure that all the children understand each teaching point. It can help to do an individual demonstration and also to add in lots of commentary about what is going on.

Children who have a sight problem rely more heavily upon their hearing to make sense of what is going on around them. Remember that children with a sight problem may also not wish to wear a swimming hat as this may muffle what they can hear.

Some children with a sight problem dislike changing in a communal changing room as they feel that everyone is watching them as the one who is different. It is good to explain that many young people feel self-conscious and most are concentrating hard on getting changed themselves as quickly as possible. Some young people may benefit from support to improve their dressing and self-care skills so that they can change quickly and confidently alongside their peers.

It is not uncommon for children to try so hard that they are not relaxed in the water, with the result that they are "fighting" with the water instead of gliding through it. It can be helpful to use commentary to encourage a child to use slower more purposeful strokes.

Encouragement and praise

© Clive Spencer

It is important that swimming sessions are positive and fun. This can be achieved by creating an atmosphere that includes fun and laughter. Activities should include an element of play with others. Praising children for having a go helps to build the children's confidence in the water. Every achievement, however small should be acknowledged and praised. This is particularly important for children with a sight problem who may be less aware of their own progress.

Giving plenty of feedback helps all the children to develop an understanding of their ability, as well as helping them develop the vocabulary of body parts, position, direction and speed. Encourage children to see how quietly and smoothly they can move through the water.

Racer

It is possible for a swimmer with little or no sight to progress to the advanced stage in swimming of tumble turns, diving and all the other skills needed in racing. A helper may tap the swimmer on the head with a foam ball on the end of a stick to tell them when to turn, although in competitions it is not acceptable to communicate with participants in any other way. This takes good timing. Here training and talking together is the best way to ensure good progress.

Other opportunities

Once a swimmer is confident the usual certificates can be taken to enable the child to get a measure of their achievement. Awards start with simple skills tests, then personal survival, and progress through to challenges. The tests that require a swimmer to be fully clothed can be very physically demanding. However the experience can be useful if a young person is interested in trying other water sports, as some ask for evidence that a person can swim in clothes. Others ask for evidence that certain distances have been achieved.

There is no reason why a child with a sight problem cannot take part in sailing, canoeing, wind surfing and water skiing with appropriate support and in a safe environment. As with learning any new skill, people are nervous at first and start off in a small way and build on their ability. To me it is like learning to ski - everyone starts off on the nursery slopes and builds up to the more difficult when they are ready! A risk assessment should always

be carried out when a child or young person is starting a new water sport, or progressing to a new environment (for example from canoeing in a swimming pool to canoeing on open water) or where new skills and activities are being introduced. Teaching children to swim is great for all round fitness and opens up all sorts of possibilities for later life, as well as helping them to enjoy more demanding physical school trips, which offer excellent opportunities for teamwork and friendship.

Dina Murdie
Former PE Teacher, RNIB New College (now retired)

■ Case study

I trained a swimmer with a sight problem who never mastered the front crawl leg kick but was very good at breaststroke. She gradually learnt to cover up the fact that she could not coordinate the free style leg kick very well and compensated by using her arms very well indeed.

To begin with, some coaches would not look at her, as front crawl is the basic training stroke. However, she had an amazing personality and was extremely persistent. As fast as "they" said she was not a swimmer, she proved them wrong by beating everyone with her breaststroke, gradually adding the other strokes as her technique improved. It was a privilege to coach her - she eventually made the Paralympic team and won medals there.

Teaching PE at GCSE

As a support teacher, it was with some apprehension that I started Year 10 with Martin. He had chosen to do GCSE PE. I knew that he enjoyed PE lessons but had not expected him to select this option. How would he cope as a pupil without vision doing such a practical course in a mainstream school?

I liaised with the PE staff prior to September about approaches. They had always been positive about including Martin in lessons and were enthusiastic about him doing GCSE. They had worked with Martin for three years, knew what he was capable of, respected his will to do as much as he could and responded positively. Martin's attitude to PE of "give everything a try", had encouraged their positive approach.

In theory

For the theory part of the course (50 per cent) the PE staff were extremely organised. They gave me a file containing handouts, worksheets and lesson plans for the whole of the two years. Such organisation on their part made my life much easier. I knew where we were heading, and had clear ideas about what would need to be brailled, to be put onto tape, or made into tactile diagrams for each lesson.

Martin enjoyed theory lessons. With support, he was able to overcome most difficulties. He had already studied the skeletal and cardio-vascular systems in biology and found these aspects straightforward. Other areas covered included the muscular system, body types, training and diet. He was more efficient at writing using his braille notetaker than the rest of the group were at making written notes and often finished before the teacher had written everything on the board.

Martin did not like tactile diagrams, however. He would take one look and then dismiss them saying, "They are just a load of lines to me." He found 3-D models or using his own body to identify relevant muscles or bones more useful. Some one-to-one follow up time from Visual Impairment staff was essential after lessons to ensure notes were in order and concepts understood. Notes were then put onto audiocassette for revision purposes.

Assessment

Along with the PE staff I attended a training day organised by the examinations board, Edexcel, on assessment for pupils with disabilities. The examiner did not have all the answers but was open to suggestions about ways forward and very much wanted to encourage students with disbabilities to do the course.

One area of concern was whether we assessed Martin against a universal standard of sporting excellence from the sighted world, or looked at his considerable sporting prowess in the context of his disability. Thankfully, Edexcel took the latter approach. A pupil without sight would not be expected, for example, to display good hand-eye coordination in basketball (as mentioned in the marking scheme). It was also agreed to be too dangerous to put a student without vision into a tough contact sport such as rugby.

However, certain principles were retained. Martin had to be assessed in ball games and striking games. We considered asking Edexcel whether goalball (see page 35) would be an acceptable sport for Martin to do but Martin decided not to choose this, so we concentrated on mainstream sports.

Practical matters

Wherever possible Martin was included fully in the practical lesson. This was no problem in sports where individual performance was assessed, such as athletics, swimming and gymnastics, as long as support staff were able to keep up with him.

In team games a number of adaptations were needed. We reduced the number of players in the game, used sound beacons in striking games, increased the ball size, used bell balls, reduced the size of the playing area (eg used a squash court) or, if absolutely necessary, concentrated on the skills of the game rather than the game itself.

One challenge we had was how to model the techniques involved in various sports. Martin had never seen anybody serve in tennis, throw a javelin or bowl in cricket. The PE staff were excellent at using Martin as a model to demonstrate skills to the rest of the group. There would then be considerable one-to-one follow up by me. This worked particularly well in swimming and, as a consequence, Martin was one of the few pupils in the group to develop good butterfly technique.

Transparency with the rest of the class about Martin's assessment was essential. He had represented England in an international athletics tournament for people with visual impairment but was considerably slower at 100 metres than most of the rest of the class. Technique and style were just as important as speed in the assessment, however, and getting all the class involved in assessing each other and working on each other's technique was a way to overcome any uncertainty over this.

Some adapting and interpreting of the existing marking criteria to Martin's situation had to be done. We looked at how much he had improved in particular skills. In hockey Martin was able to participate in small group games and had developed good skills at shooting and dribbling by the end of the course. In basketball he was able to play one-on-one against another player and had developed good technique at various shots and good ball control. We felt that he had improved more in basketball than in hockey and, consequently, he got a higher grade in this.

Examination

At the end of year 11 Martin took the exam. The theory paper was in braille and he had a practical assessment by the school, externally moderated. The examiner saw him in swimming and basketball. Martin was able to tell the examiner how to do a Jump Shot. He then demonstrated one and got it into the basket first time. In the end he attained a Grade B. He felt disappointed at this but the grade was a good reflection of his efforts and enthusiasm over the two years. Asking him about it a few months later he said that he had thoroughly enjoyed the course too.

The apprehension I had felt at the start of the course had been unnecessary. With liaison, planning and the goodwill of the PE staff, the two years had proved to be a resounding success.

Phil Sutcliffe
Walsall Visual Impairment Service

This article is based upon an article, "Teaching PE at GCSE" which was first published in RNIB's education magazine Visability, Spring 2003.

Case study

Hassan, Year 8 onwards - Coping with senior school PE

Hassan has myopia (very short sight), a retinal detachment in his right eye, and a limited field of vision on his right side. He can see at 6 metres what a fully sighted person can see at 36 metres.

Hassan has always been thoroughly involved in PE and he was particularly keen on sport when he was in the primary school. He was socially well integrated and successfully worked with the other children. He did not like having assistance from a member of the support staff, although the class teacher requested that she join Hassan for certain activities, where she simply supervised certain safety situations.

During his first two years at secondary school Hassan took part in all the sports. However it was decided that rugby and basketball were too dangerous to continue with, bearing in mind any bump on the head may aggravate his retinal problem and he could end up losing the sight altogether in his right eye.

Difficulties arising in the teenage years

1 Hassan's problems first started when he realised that there was a much greater competitive element to sport generally in secondary school. His peer group from the primary school was not so inclined to bowl a "slow" ball in cricket or send a "gentle" pass in football. The new friends that Hassan made from other primary feeder schools simply did not understand his sight problems and were less inclined to be sympathetic towards his needs.

2 Towards the end of Year 8 Hassan realised that other boys were developing much greater strength and speed and he began to get despondent because he could not keep up with them.

3 Hassan was somewhat annoyed when it was decided that he should, for safety reasons, have to give up rugby and basketball.

Suggestions for overcoming difficulties in Year 9 onwards

Although there should continue to be an element of "competition", pupils with sight problems often find it much easier to succeed in individual sports rather than team sports. For example, when Hassan gave up basketball and rugby he joined another group of pupils who were doing gymnastics and swimming.

Considerable persuasive and coercive efforts were needed to encourage Hassan to accept an alternative activity.

Eventually a sixth form student was engaged, rather then a member of the Learning Support staff, to become involved with recording, monitoring and giving some support and assistance. This was only given in the presence of and under the guidance of the PE staff.

When Hassan arrived at the situation where he had to choose PE options in Year 11 he chose to work in the "Fitness" area. Appropriate supervision was available but Hassan had already undergone a thorough initiation both in Year 10 with the school class and also when he joined the local community centre session that was held there in the evening. Hassan was therefore able to work with confidence in this area.

Hassan eventually accepted that although he had enjoyed team sports in the primary school he now looked forward to a range of individual challenges that were more appropriate for his vision.

Increasingly secondary schools are acquiring multigym equipment such as running, cycling and rowing machines, and resistance machines and weights to aid muscle tone and strength. In many schools there is insufficient equipment for large groups but these facilities can be extremely useful in helping a young person with a sight problem to develop their general fitness levels, in the company of a small group. It can sometimes be an attractive alternative for young people with sight problems who are beginning to find the pace of team games impractical and dispiriting. It is an excellent environment in which to measure and acknowledge personal achievement and progress, and the activities can be carried on into adult life. (See page 21 for more information on multigyms.)

Angela Brassey
RNIB Advisory Teacher of Visually Impaired Children, PE and Mobility
RNIB New College Worcester

Equipment

The following items have been recommended to us by staff in supporting a child with sight problems taking part in PE lessons. To suggest further resources or advice on how to enable a child to participate please contact:

Suzy McDonald, RNIB Curriculum Information Officer, 58-72 John Bright Street, Birmingham B1 1BN
Tel: 0121 665 4223 Fax: 0121 665 4201
Email: suzy.mcdonald@rnib.org.uk

Prices and availability are subject to change.

Balls

Spordas Spider Ball

Spider balls are made of solid rubber and have "legs" protruding from all sides to make them easier to catch and stop them rolling too far if dropped. Very popular with children of all ages. From Davies.

Spordas Sensi-Ball

This ball, with a gently bumpy outer surface, is very easy to catch, hold and throw. It comes in bright yellow, and is particularly suitable for teaching throwing and catching skills to children who have sight problems. Set of two from Davies.

Spordas Sof-Stuf

Sof-Stuf balls come in a variety of sizes and shapes and are soft and brightly coloured. Highly visible and durable. From Davies.

Balzac Balloon Ball

A novel idea, which has proved popular in a number of mainstream school settings. You insert a balloon into the cloth cover and inflate. The result is a durable but very light ball, which can be safely kicked or hit. From Davies.

Cloth covered Low-Bounce ball

This ball has a soft, slow bounce and is covered with multi-coloured panels, which makes it easier to spot. Ideal for children with sight problems of all ages. From Davies.

Koosh Ball

Ever popular, these balls are ideal for developing basic hand-eye co-ordination. They are made from thousands of rubber band-like tentacles and don't bounce or roll. From Davies.

Spordas Jingle Trainer

This lightweight ball contains metal bells that are suspended inside the ball, so that it jingles when moved. Perfect for most ball sports with children who are blind or partially sighted, and light enough for children to play safely. From Davies.

Gym and Playball

This rubber ball has bells inside and is suitable for water games. From RNIB.

Audible Mitre Football

This football is made from inflatable rubber and contains metal pieces which rattle when the football is shaken or moved. From RNIB.

Football coaching video

This video is made by the manager of the England Blind Football Team, Tony Larkin. It introduces football coaches to the principles of coaching players who are blind. Approximate cost £15, produced by Sporting Solutions Ltd. Available from Tony Fitzsimmons on 07751 079235 or sportingsolutions@hotmail.com

Football for players with sight problems

This specially designed audible football has multiple interior compartments to maximise the sound and its audible responsiveness to movement. Costs approximately £15 from Tony Fitzsimmons on 07751 079235 or sportingsolutions@hotmail.com

Goalball

This ball, used to play the popular game of Goalball, is available from British Blind Sport for £35.

Teamster plastic balls

These small lightweight plastic balls can be easily adapted for children who have sight problems with the purchase of a few bells, available from sewing suppliers. These bells were referred to by the PE curriculum group as "Morris Dancer" bells. They come in sizes small enough to insert through the holes in the teamster balls. Once in, they do not come out but give an effective jingle when rattled. From Davies in packs of 12.

Other equipment

Kickmaster

The Kickmaster is a net on an adjustable retractable cord which will extend, by way of a button/trigger on the handle, to a maximum of 4.3m. The audible mitre football is ideal for use with the Kickmaster to practise soccer skills. From ToysRUs.

Spordas Direct Cue Lines and Corners

These throw down vinyl lines which stick temporarily to the floor are great for use with children who have sight problems. Made from 3mm thick vinyl, with bevelled edges, they are useful for teaching position to blind and partially sighted children as they can feel the lines and borders of play areas. From Davies.

Spordas Sequencing Spots

These vinyl discs in bright colours are also very useful for teaching positioning skills for sport and athletic activities. From Davies.

Coloured Balance Benches

These balance benches are traditionally constructed in high quality pine, with a painted double layer and laquered for a long lasting finish. Particularly suitable for children who have very little sight, who can see colour contrasts as these benches are more likely to be a different colour to the gym or exercise hall floor. Alternatively, mark up traditional wooden benches with bright, contrasting tape (available in red, yellow, blue or white). Available in in red, blue, green or yellow from Davies.

Brightly coloured mats

Davies offers a range of brightly coloured mats. These are ideal for marking out boundaries for games with pupils of all ages and abilities. Choose colours that contrast with the floor of your gym.

Up Rite Safe Tee

Great for batting practice, the weighted base in this batting tee allows it to rock forward if hit then return automatically to its upright position. The height is adjustable and is especially suitable if used with a ball in a contrasting colour. From Davies.

Coloured skipping ropes

2.4m lightweight plaited skipping ropes with handles are available in 6 colours, red, yellow, blue, green, purple and orange. From Davies.

Team bands

The coloured bands used to identify team members are ideal for use as guide ropes between a pupil with a sight problem and a sighted guide. Link the two people by looping the band around each wrist - ideal for exercises such as running. Available from Davies.

Tactile and talking measuring equipment

RNIB stocks a number of products that can help a young person with a sight problem be involved in measuring their progress in athletics. For example, talking stopwatches can be used in time trials, and tactile measuring tapes and rulers, and a 5m talking tape measure are useful for measuring the outcomes of jumping and throwing events. For up to date prices and more details about the products visit www.onlineshop.rnib.org.uk or telephone RNIB Customer Services on 0845 7023153.

Water-based equipment

PVC logs

These floating polyethylene logs are great for giving water confidence, and come in bright primary colours, making them particularly suitable for children with some colour recognition. From Davies.

Funnoodles

These flexible giant tubes in primary colours measure 165cm in length and have a diameter of 7cm. Flexible enough to wrap around waists, they are great fun for children of all swimming abilities. From Davies.

Frog board

With bright green and yellow sides, the floating frog boards give children more confidence in the pool and are big enough to support the body weight of children. Available in two sizes from Davies.

Suppliers

RNIB Customer Services, PO Box 173, Peterborough PE2 6WS
(for the price of a local call)
Tel: 0845 7023153

Davies Sports, Findel House, Excelsior Road, Ashby Park, Ashby-de-la-Zouch, Leicestershire LE65 1NG
Tel: 0845 1204 515

British Blind Sport
(see page 50 for contact details)

Please note it is likely that you can get similar equipment from other sports equipment manufacturers and local sports shops.

Useful contacts

Where do you go to find out about sport for people with sight problems? Here are some very useful organisations that can help you get started.

National contacts

Action for Blind People (AFBP) Actionnaires Clubs

Throughout the UK many blind and partially sighted children and young people struggle to be meaningfully involved in sporting activities at school. Action for Blind People's Actionnaires clubs aim to get them off the sideline and onto the pitch!

Our seven clubs across the UK, located in areas where there is a lack of local service provision, are regularly attended by over 150 children with sight problems, their siblings and friends.

For the children and young people aged 8-16 who attend, the clubs not only offer sporting opportunities but also the chance to develop their confidence and social skills. A range of sporting options is available including archery, athletics, basketball, cricket, football, goalball, judo, martial arts and parachute games.

The success of the clubs relies on close partnership working. The team works hard to develop local links with volunteer and coaching bodies, sporting venues and partner organisations in the visual impairment field. Actionnaires clubs are kindly supported by BBC Children in Need and The Primary Club.

To find out more about the locations, times and activities offered by our Actionnaires clubs please contact:

Sports Development Officer South
Tel: 020 7635 4905

Sports Development Officer North
Tel: 01772 555915

Visit Action for Blind People's website at www.afbp.org/sports

Or call Action for Blind People's Freephone Helpline on 0800 915 4666

British Blind Sport (BBS)

BBS is the co-ordinating body for blind sport in the UK. They have a number of sports sub-committees who organise competitions and squad-training sessions.

BBS is a membership organisation and would be able to assist you in finding a sports club. They also have an excellent website, www.britishblindsport.org.uk that provides detailed information about a variety of sports that people with sight problems participate in.

British Blind Sport
4-6 Victoria Terrace
Leamington Spa
CV31 3AB

Tel: 01926 424247

English Federation of Disability Sport (EFDS)

EFDS is the national body responsible for developing sport for disabled people in England. They have regional officers who would be able to assist you with identifying sporting opportunities for yourself. Their website address is www.efds.co.uk or you can contact them at their national office:

English Federation of Disability Sport
Alsager Campus
Manchester Metropolitan University
Hassall Road
Alsager ST7 2HL

Tel: 0161 247 5294

Federation of Disability Sport Wales

National governing body for disability sport in Wales, delivering a community participation scheme as well as elite programming through to paralympic games.

c/o Sports Council for Wales
Sophia Gardens
Cardiff
CF11 9SW

Tel: 02920 300526

Scottish Disability Sport

Head Office
The Administrator
Scottish Disability Sport
Caledonia House
South Gyle
Edinburgh EH12 9DQ

Tel: 0131 317 1130

Disability Sports Northern Ireland

Disability Sports Northern Ireland
Unit 10
Ormeau Business Park
8 Cromac Avenue
Belfast BT7 2JA

Tel: 028 9050 8255
Email: email@dsni.co.uk

PE Curriculum Group

Teachers may be interested to know of the existence of the PE Curriculum Group of VIEW/RNIB which meets twice a year to discuss and co-ordinate matters of common interest to PE teachers of children and young people who have sight problems.

For further details, please contact:
Angela Beach
St Vincents School
Yew Tree Lane, West Derby
Liverpool L12 9HN

Tel: 0151 228 9968

Judo

Peter Topping 1st DAN
Judo Coach for the Visually Impaired

Tel: 0161 881 0523
Email: manchester.judo@ntlworld.com

British Judo Association

7A Rutland Street
Leicester LE1 1RB

Tel: 0116 255 9669
Email: bja@britishjudo.org.uk
Website: www.britishjudo.org.uk

Manchester Judo Society and DOJO

Email: manchester.judo@ntlworld.com

National Blind Children's Society holiday schemes

The National Blind Children's Society runs a "School's Out" programme of Activity Weeks, throughout the UK. The weeks enable children and young people with sight problem to socialise with their peers at the same time as developing their independence. Challenging activities are offered in safe, secure and structured environments to give children and young people with visual impairment opportunities to experience and enjoy outdoor activities in recognised activity centres. Further details are available from Glenys Critchley.

Email: Glenys.critchley@nbcs.org.uk

RNIB Vacation Schemes

RNIB Vacation Schemes provide a one week residential holiday experience for children and young people with sight problems. The holidays are designed to meet the social needs of children and young people aged 8-17 years who attend mainstream schools. Children with sight problems sometimes struggle to be fully included in leisure opportunities at school and in their local community. RNIB Vacation Schemes offer a tailor-made leisure programme of valuable social and recreational opportunities.

RNIB Vacation Schemes enable young people to:

- spend time with other children and young people who have a sight problem. For many this will be their first opportunity to do so

- meet new challenges and try new leisure activities in a safe and supportive environment; to set their own level of challenge for each activity, ensuring each individual maximises their personal achievement

- increase their personal independence and life skills

- experience opportunities for extending their social skills.

We work with families after the event to support them in accessing information about leisure opportunities and to help young people to get involved in mainstream leisure activities closer to home.

The Vacation Scheme brochure is produced each year at the beginning of January. To register for a free copy please contact the Leisure Services Administrator on Telephone 0113 274 8855 or at RNIB, Grosvenor House, Grosvenor Road, Headingley, Leeds LS6 2DZ. Alternatively email LeisureServices@rnib.org.uk

RNIB Vocational College, Loughborough

RNIB Vocational College, Loughborough offers academic and vocational training for people with disabilities. Loughborough is famous for sport, and Vocational College is no exception, their football team have regular success in the British Blind Sports league and five goalball players have trained with the national team. Contact the college for further information:

Tel: 01509 61 10 77
Email: enquiries@rnibvocoll.ac.uk
Website: www.rnibvocoll.ac.uk

Local level

Contact your local authority sports development unit. They should be able to give details of local sports clubs in your area. They may have an officer specifically designated for disabled people, and details of sports opportunities specifically for young people with disabilities.

There are some local sports clubs for people with sight problems too. Contact BBS for details of clubs in your area or contact your local organisations for people who are blind or partially sighted.

Regional support

You could contact a regional organisation. For example, in London, the London Sports Forum for Disabled People co-ordinates sports opportunities for disabled people in London.

For further information, see www.londonsportsforum.org.uk

They can also offer advice on making sport accessible to people with sight problems. For example, by advising on appropriate equipment and/or amendments to mainstream sports so that people with sight problems can take part. There are similar organisations in other parts of the country.

Contact the relevant national organisations listed on pages 50 and 51 for regional contact details.

Further information

RNIB Family Services

RNIB's Family Support Officers offer advice and support to children with sight problems, their siblings and their families, and also to professionals working with children with sight problems. They work in partnership with the statutory and voluntary sector, developing and delivering a range of events, as well as increasing or supporting access to existing leisure and social activities. For further information contact Kathleen O'Gorman, Family Services Development Officer on 0151 298 3222.

RNIB Visability magazine

An education magazine for professionals and families supporting children and young people who have sight problems. Visability contains practical ideas and advice from practitioners across mainstream settings about issues such as mobility and independence, technology, accessing the curriculum, and the latest research and literature. Parents also regularly share their own experiences. An annual subscription (3 issues) costs £10.50 (UK) and £15 (overseas). Various formats. More information from RNIB Customer Services Tel: 0845 702 3153.

RNIB Book Sales Service

RNIB Book Sales Service is the UK's leading publisher and distributor of publications from the UK, Europe and the rest of the world on education and employment in the field of sight loss including additional disabilities. Over 450 titles are available via mail order including books, videos and other materials. To order a free catalogue, contact RNIB Customer Services on 0845 702 3153 Email: cservices@rnib.org.uk, quoting ED001.

RNIB Online Shop

Over 800 products and publications are available to buy online including publications from RNIB Book Sales Service.

Website: http://onlineshop.rnib.org.uk

Index